AF802971

The Magic of Spinning

The Magic of Spinning

Wool Wheel

HOW TO DO IT YOURSELF, WITH THE EMPHASIS ON WOOL, THE HISTORY OF SPINNING, AND OTHER FACTS.

BY MARION L. CHANNING
Illustrated by Walter E. Channing
35 Main Street, Marion, Massachusetts

COPYRIGHT © 1966, 1967, 1969, 1971, 1975
MARION L. CHANNING, MARION, MASSACHUSETTS

All rights reserved. Parts or all of this book may not be reproduced by any means without permission in writing from the copyright owner, in care of the publisher.

Library of Congress Catalog Card Number 72-180769
ISBN 0-9600496-0-6
SIXTH PRINTING

Also by
MARION L. CHANNING

"THE TEXTILE TOOLS OF COLONIAL HOMES"
"A LITTLE ABOUT LACE"

"LAURA RUSSELL REMEMBERS"
with notes by
MARION L. CHANNING

Published by
The Channings
Box 552
Marion, Massachusetts 02738

Printed by
Reynolds-DeWalt Printing, Inc.
New Bedford, Massachusetts

Contents

PREFACE TO THE SECOND EDITION

(With Helpful Hints)

Let me recommend writing a book as a way to increase one's horizons in a fascinating manner. The first edition of this book has brought me new friends and experiences little suspected when I first went to the printer. From these associations I have gathered little bits of supplementary information which have come my way.

First of all I would like to thank Paula Simmons of Suquamish, Washington for all the help and encouragement she has given me, including the weekly (often more) letters she has written, and for the publicity campaign she has carried on in behalf of spinning with the book profiting by it.

She and her husband raise their own sheep, and through the most careful breeding have developed a flock which yields fleeces in all shades of lovely browns, blacks, and greys. (As the sheep grow older in years they lighten.) Paula is a true artist, the kind who sets her standards high. In fact, she nails them to the masthead! The results are reflected in the yarn she spins (a beauty treatment for knitters' hands in addition to being of the highest quality). This yarn she then weaves into materials which have gained for her many well earned prizes at Fairs and Shows. Mrs. Simmons has made the once lowly craft of spinning an art.

I am very grateful to my husband who has drawn with meticulous care the new pictures which will add helpful and interesting information.

Our new illustrations show spindles for the wool wheel, (though it was used for cotton spinning in the South.) The direct drive, or bat head, was in use for centuries. In 1802 Amos Minor of Marcellus, New York patented the "Improved and Warranted Accelerating Wheel Head" which he had invented. This of course speeds up the spinning which was so necessary at the time. However, some modern spinners feel that it is too swift, making the yarn a bit hard to control.

Another new drawing shows clearly how the spindle fits into the leather bearings on the maidens of the flax wheel. I have seen this

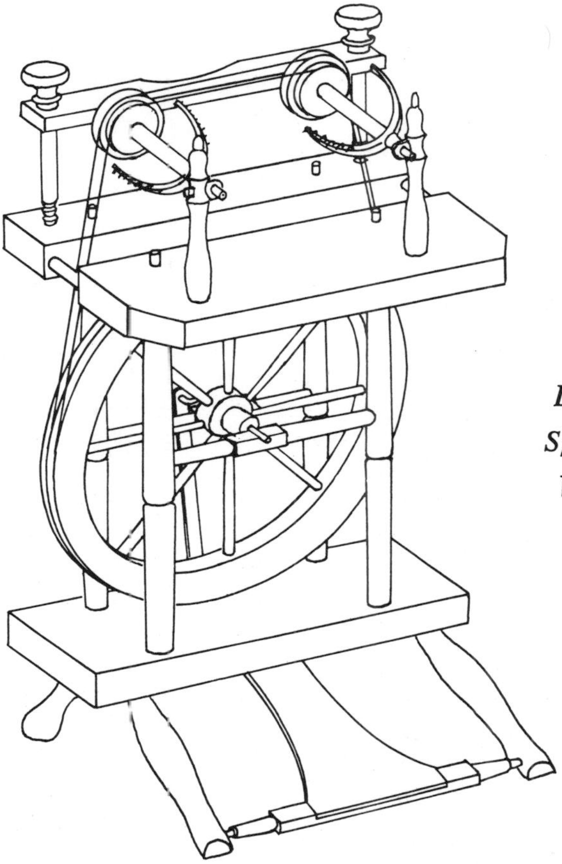

Double Spinning Wheel

spindle inserted directly into the maidens both in a wheel in a private home and in a large museum. The idle visitor does not know the difference, but of course it is impossible to spin with it in this position.

The Scandinavians position their spindles in one or both maidens in their modern wheels. But the holes go all the way through, leaving access to the orifice.

The wool wheel was also called a walking wheel due to the walking involved. The castle wheel is also known as a cottage wheel. A glance at the drawing of the double flax wheel on page five will explain its other names, gossip wheel and lovers' wheel. It is possible for two people to operate this at once, one or two pedalling, and using wool and/or flax. Or one can use it, but the quality is not the best. It would also be interesting to know the quality of the yarn spun by the Egyptians shown on a tomb about 1900 B.C. Men and women are both shown spinning (whorl near top of spindle), and women are using two spindles at once. Try it some time!

Those with limited time and facilities sometimes purchase from woolen mills top for spinning. This of course saves time and a lot of hard work, but one does not get the same satisfaction when the wool is processed by hand from the beginning. In starting with the fleece, complete control of every step is possible, thereby obtaining a superior product.

In reviewing the subject of washing, these points stand out. Wool must be treated with respect and care. Be gentle. Rough washing is out. Be sure the soap is completely dissolved in the water before putting the wool in. And don't run the rinse water on the wool.

The final use of the yarn determines many factors in washing. Before uncarded wool or yarn is dyed, it is necessary to do a very thorough job of removing the grease. The spinner must decide for himself about water temperature, soap or detergent. A little experimenting will bring forth the best solution. Yarn should also be washed before using anyway. Dyeing in a carded batt can sadly mat the wool.

There appear to be different theories on how much wool to put on a card before carding. As in many things, one has to use good judgment. The height of the teeth actually determines the amount. Old cards have them set close to the leather, while the new ones I have observed are higher. Obviously a thin layer on high teeth is going to be a struggle. A little experimenting will show the correct amount for your own cards.

Mrs. John Scammell of Brimfield, Massachusetts uses these key words in teaching others to spin. 1. Pinch. 2. Pull. 3. Release. The left hand pinches the yarn where it becomes loose wool. The right hand pulls out some wool while controlling the unspun, so that the twist does not race through the large mass. Then the left hand releases so that the twist can go along the pulled out unspun wool, but not into the mass. Now start over. Get someone to turn the wheel very slowly for you, and don't use short fiber wool. The same method holds for spindle spinning.

Even though many of our readers will never spin, it is good to just know about its' history and theories, and it helps us to appreciate our ancestors and their textiles. To would-be spinners, good luck with your yarn and the product you make from it.

Dedication

To Alberta S. Belden, whose integrity and hard work for her family will never be forgotten, and to John A. Belden, whose interest in my projects helped to make this book possible.

AFTER my mother passed away, I had the great pleasure of helping my father in his antique business. One of the treasures that he acquired was a tremendous loom of the Pre-Revolutionary War Period which he found in pieces lying in a snow drift. Being eager to learn to weave, I enlisted the aid of my husband who is mechanically inclined. Soon this gigantic machine was operational, though we had made many preliminary mistakes.

Of course the next step to weaving was spinning, and I looked longingly at a big wool wheel which came into my father's shop. But how to learn to spin? Later this problem was solved (after the wheel was sold) when the New Hampshire League of Arts and Crafts had demonstrations of spinning at its 1964 summer fair. At this fair I talked to one of the spinners who encouraged me to learn. Immediately upon arriving home, I went to my father's attic and brought down the flax wheel which had been waiting patiently for me these hundred years or more. He remembered it stored away in his boyhood home with no one able to use it. But typical of New Englanders, it was never thrown away. Where it originally came from, and when it was last used, history does not tell. It was in excellent condition, needing only a new driving band.

From this start my spinning adventures began. First of all I sought out some wool at a time when most of it had gone to the wool pool. Talking with spinners at Old Sturbridge Village and elsewhere, I learned the basic techniques. The few books on the subject were also very helpful.

All the while in my father's travels searching for his beloved Early Americana, he picked up spinning equipment, including a double flax wheel. These miscellaneous items were added to the collection in his living room where the loom had finally landed. I don't know any other father who would have enjoyed such chaos. But enjoy it he did, and I shall always be eternally grateful to him.

Foreword

THERE are as many ideas on spinning as there are spinners. These ideas are often contradictory, and it is quite possible that you, the reader, may differ with me. In any case, I would like to hear from you. On the whole I have tried to present all viewpoints in an unbiased manner. As to method, you be the judge as to the right one for you. I have also checked and double checked my information hoping to be as accurate as possible.

In addition to the instructions in spinning, I am including a bit of history, and how the craft was related to everyday life in the Colonies. This knowledge makes us more appreciative of spinning. Other information is included for the would-be (and can-be) spinner.

The emphasis is on wool rather than flax, because there are many hand knitters as well as weavers who use hand spun wool. Fewer people use their own linen, although not too many years ago it had many uses. One of the spinners at Old Sturbridge Village, Mrs. Scammell, writes me that:

"As recently as my mother's girlhood, summer stockings were knitted of bleached hand spun linen yarn. Also lace was knitted and crocheted from linen as trimming for pillow cases, summer draws, petticoats, lamp mats, bureau scarves, and whole bedspreads."

Essentially flax spinning is the same as wool in method. However, it is necessary to prepare a distaff and dampen the fibers as it is being spun in order to control it. There is also a dry spin method. Converting the flax plant to a useable fiber is also difficult, tedious, and not to be undertaken lightly. In fact, it is hard work!

Even if you never plan to become a spinner, I hope you will find the subject as interesting as I have. The books I have read and the museums I have visited are well worth the time, and I would commend them to your attention whenever possible.

Acknowledgements

"My help cometh from the Lord, which made heaven and earth."
Psalm 121:2.

I AM also very grateful for the gracious and constructive assistance I have received from the right people at the right time and at the right place. Included among these are the spinners at the Craftsmen's Fairs and at Old Sturbridge Village (especially Mrs. John Scammell). Mrs. Philip Gibbs of Locust Lea Farm, Carver, Massachusetts has talked to me at great length about the raising of sheep. Mrs. Harold C. Goddard, the assistant librarian at Merrimack Valley Textile Museum, North Andover, Massachusetts knew just the books that would be most helpful in research. A retired textile school teacher, who prefers to remain anonymous, has been of great assistance in checking the technical details. Mr. S. W. Bridges, Marion, Massachusetts has discussed wool with me from the manufacturer's point of view. Many thanks to all of you.

My apologies go to the grammarians who may read this, their polished rhetoric being beyond the reach of my housewife English.

The following books were invaluable.

Colonial Living, Edwin Tunis, The World Publishing Co., 1957.

Home Life in Colonial Days, Alice Morse Earle, Grosset & Dunlap, 1898.

How to Know Textiles, Cassie Paine Small, Ginn and Co., Boston, 1925.

Sheep Science, William Garfield Kammlade, Sr. and Jr., J. B. Lippincott Co., Chicago, 1955.

The Tale of the Spinning Wheel, Elizabeth Cynthia Barney Buel, 1903.

Textiles, Woolman and McGowan, The Macmillan Co., New York, 1938.

Wool Technology and the Industrial Revolution, Merrimack Valley Textile Museum, North Andover, Massachusetts, 1965.

The World Book Encyclopedia, Field Enterprises Educational Corporation, Chicago, Illinois, 1955.

Your Handspinning, Elsie G. Davenport, Craft and Hobby Book Service, Big Sur, California, 1964.

CHAPTER I

History through the Ages

NO one knows exactly where or when the art of spinning first appeared, although it is known that even in the Early Stone Age this art was well advanced. Man had gradually given up his nomadic life, and his demands for household goods had increased. He had learned to cultivate plants and to domesticate animals. In fact, wool from sheep might well have been the earliest fiber used in spinning, since it was readily available. Fibers from plants such as flax and cotton were undoubtedly known and cultivated at an early time. Certain it is that flax was in use before the age of metals previous to 5000 B. C. Bits of flax and flax yarn have been found in primitive homes which were dug from deep under the mud of Swiss lakes. (A strong witness for the durability of linen!)

As ancient as is the art of spinning, weaving with its readily available materials in the form of twigs and grasses, probably came first in the textile arts. Also preceeding spinning was dyeing if Greek mythology can be said to have a chronological sequence. (Even in prehistoric times man enjoyed bright and interesting colors.)

The dyer Idmon was the father of Arachne, a spinner. Ovid tells the story of how she challenged Pallas Athene, whose godly interests included spinning, and who acknowledged no superior in gods or man. The goddess disguised herself as an old woman and attempted to discourage the foolish girl from the contest. But to no avail. Arachne was defeated and in her shame she hanged herself. Athene pitied her and said,

"Live, and that you may preserve the memory of this lesson, continue to hang, both you and your descendents, to all future times."

This is the mythological beginning of spiders whose family name is arachnid.

The art and history of dyeing is a story all its own, one we will not delve into here.

In the evolution of spinning the same three steps are always involved. 1. Attenuate or draw out the fibers. 2. Twist them, 3. Wind them up. And so this same method was used in the very beginning when only the fingers were used. After the fiber was twisted, it was necessary to roll it in a ball or wind it onto a stick. This stick was spun to help the twisting. As the yarn built up, it must have been noticed that it spun around better. This in turn led to adding the whorl near the bottom of the stick. Most of the time it had a notch at the top to catch the spun yarn and hold it securely.

Cloth found in Egyptian tombs dating from around 4000 B. C. can not be surpassed today. It was dyed, and the spinning and weaving are superb. Some of the earliest examples of cloth come from India where cotton spinning regulations, or specifications were drawn up about 1000 B. C. Silk was made into cloth in China and Japan at the dawn of their history.

The great early writer, Homer, mentions spinners and their gorgeous wools, and legend tells that even Hercules spun for love of Omphale. Shakespeare, himself, remarks with a humor we can enjoy today that Penelope was a diligent spinner.

"All the yarn she spun in Ulysses' absence did but fill Ithaca full of moths."

In the Old Testament days we read in Proverbs of the role of women in early civilization:

31:13. *"She seeketh wool and flax, and worketh willingly with her hands."*

31:19. *"She layeth her hands to the spindle, and her hands hold the distaff."*

31:24. *"She maketh fine linen, and selleth it; and delivereth girdles unto the merchant."*

In South America, after the time of Christ the Incas and Mayans produced beautiful materials. The Spanish explorers found cloth in the New World whose colors rivaled those of Europe in beauty and fastness.

Even in a distant North American outpost, spinning was a vital part of living. A Norwegian archeologist working in Newfoundland in the summer of 1962 uncovered an ancient Norse settlement. One of the artifacts found was a part from a wool spinning spindle, which resembled those found in ancient Scandinavia. Using the carbon 14 method of dating, the Viking village is thought to be about the year 1000. (This coincides with the Viking sagas which tell of the early attempts to colonize in North America.)

At an early period India progressed from the spindle to the Jersey, Great, or Wool Wheel as it was called in England. Europe may have adopted this idea. Anyway, in the 14th century it began to take the place of the spindle there. Actually the large wheel was a better mechanical way of turning the spindle whose whorl had a groove in it for the belt which transferred the motion from the wheel. The motion of the great wheel is intermittent — stop and go — attenuating the fibers and twisting at the same time. Then a length of yarn is wound on the spindle. This involves much walking on the part of the spinster who might go twenty miles a day in colonial times, but more often from twelve to fifteen.

The Saxony, Brunswick, or flax wheel on which any fiber can be spun is said to have been invented by Jurgens in Germany about 1530. But it was probably around before then. Leonardo Da Vinci who lived from 1452 to 1519 is credited with inventing the flyer. Instead of turning the wheel by hand, the foot operated a treadle attached to the wheel, leaving the hands free. The belt went from the wheel, around the spindle groove, back to the wheel, around the bobbin groove, and then back to its beginning. Thus in one continuous, doubled belt, the spindle and the bobbin on it were both turned. The groove on the bobbin whorl had a smaller diameter than the one of the spindle whorl, thereby causing the bobbin to go around faster than the spindle. Thus the yarn is drawn on the bobbin. A continuous motion is established, attenuating, twisting, and winding on, all at the same time — great progress in those days.

It was at this type of wheel that Romney painted Lady Hamilton since it was fashionable to spin during the latter part of the 18th century. Probably it was done as a hobby and at the whim of our fine lady. Surely she did not produce yarn in quantities, as was necessary in the far away lands of America.

After the downfall of the feudal system the ancient textile guilds, forerunners of our unions today, became influential. They trained workers and organized trade. But the guild system faded out in the 17th century, and the Industrial Revolution was soon to come. Perhaps it was unfortunate that the guilds were not around to take part in developing the textile industry with all its ramifications of working techniques and employer-employee relations. Who knows?

By the mid 1700's, times were improving a bit. Spinning and weaving were no longer done in every home. The demand for more cloth was great. Improved weaving techniques prompted better spinning methods. John Kay speeded up weaving when he invented the flying shuttle in 1733. A big spinning problem was to draw out fibers automatically and keep many spindles revolving. Inventions, improvements, and combinations of different ideas followed one after the other in the 18th century.

England was the center of these developments. In 1738 John Wyatt took out a patent which pioneered the use of rollers to attenuate the yarn. It is important today in present power spinning. He worked with Lewis Paul, and they created a revolving cylinder with teeth on it to card and prepare the raw material. This idea was claimed by James Hargreaves, who about 1765 invented the spinning jenny. It is said to be in honor of his wife Jenny, but could be a corruption of the word jinny from engine. Others say his daughter Jenny tipped over his spinning wheel. The spindle continued to rotate giving him ideas for his machine. This must have been a remarkable invention then because it aroused a great antipathy among the spinners who feared for their jobs. (Those who worry about automation now should study this era.) The machine was wrecked, and Hargreaves was cruelly beaten. He died a poor and discouraged man. However, his ideas are still in use today, even though the jenny was not greatly used in the American cotton industry.

Perhaps Richard Arkwright had a different personality. He was a clever barber who traveled in pursuit of his trade. In his journeys he could easily see the trend of the times and what other inventors were trying to do. Building on their ideas he produced about 1769 a successful machine which made a very strong yarn. His business acumen brought him success, wealth, and a knighthood from the king.

Another improvement in 1779 was made by Samuel Crompton. He called this machine a mule because it was a cross between those inventions of Hargreaves and Arkwright.

In the comparative short space of 55 years, from 1770 to 1825 spinning production went from one spinner with one wheel and spindle who could produce four skeins in a day to one spinner with one spinning jack having 140 spindles who produced 700 skeins in a day.

And so it went. The carding operation methods were improved and the material became a continuous sliver. Along with Whitney's cotton gin came Watt's steam engine. Power which was originally supplied by man had gone from water to steam, and in 1790 the latter was used for spinning. Today we look forward to universal use of nuclear power to do our work. The Industrial Revolution is indeed repeating itself in Automation now.

CHAPTER II

Spinning in Colonial Days

"And all the women that were wise-hearted did spin with their hands, and brought that which they had spun, both of blue, of purple, and of scarlet, and of fine linen." Exodus 35:25

IN 1800 there were approximately three and a half million spinning wheels in the United States. Where are they now? Undoubtedly most of them have gone up in smoke. Museums and tearooms have their share (with important parts missing!) as do modern colonial living rooms where philodendron and ivy wind around the spokes of the wheel if the children haven't been allowed to spin it constantly. But there are places where people really love to spin and do it as a useful hobby.

Spinning had always been an honorable occupation. When James 1st was presented to a young lady of great accomplishments, he wanted to know.

"Pray tell me, can she spin?"

All the spinning wheels that came over in the Mayflower would probably overflow the Queen Mary today! Who does know how many did come? The Pilgrims did bring however, valuable ideas which they picked up in their twelve year stay at Leyden in Holland.

Twenty five years after the Pilgrims landed, there were 3000 sheep in New England. This was not enough for food, and barely enough for yarn. Flax supplemented, providing linen for the warp. Linsey-woolsey was the resulting material. They needed more wool in order to clothe all that lived here then. They disliked importing clothes, which might carry disease. (This was as great a threat then as our atomic bomb is now.) It also cost money, and they were still rather poor at that time.

Many of the early settlers had made cloth at home in England and were well acquainted with the process. For color they imported indigo for blue, and, when possible, madder for red. Available here were tree bark, roots, flowers, and berries for the yellows and browns.

In 1640 the Court of Massachusetts passed a law which governed the growing of flax and which ordered that boys and girls be taught to spin. At Old Sturbridge Village they tell about girls five years old being taught this craft. Moreover, at one time in Connecticut every family was ordered to spin a certain number of pounds of flax a year or to pay a fine. Jamestown, Virginia erected two spinning schools in 1646 which were meant to serve the purpose of our present day vocational schools.

The General Court of the Massachusetts Bay Colony in 1656 found it necessary to issue this order: "All hands not necessarily employed on other occasions, as women, girls, and boys are enjoyned to spin according to their skill and ability." For a long time it was ruled that every home have one spinner. And we complain about our laws today! The men and older boys were not required to spin. They must have been much too busy preparing the flax for their sisters, mothers, and wives!

The preparing of the fibers with its many steps was difficult, and there were fewer social gatherings than there were in other occupations which made the burden seem lighter. One of these is humorously depicted in a painting in the Garbisch Collection of the National Gallery of Art, Washington, D. C. called "Flax-scutching Bee" by Linton Park in 1860. It pictures a lively scene.

The following is a brief description of the many processes involved. The flax was pulled, roots and all, from the ground, dried, rippled to remove the seeds, and then retted in a convenient pond, hence the often heard name Flax Pond. Retting is the rotting of the outside bark and woody core. After it has been thoroughly dried again, the useless part of the plant must be separated. The rotted tissue is broken to pieces on a flax brake. Further scutching or swingling knocks off the bits of straw. Then it is hackled according to how fine a fiber is needed. This is done by drawing the material through a set of steel teeth. Finally it is ready for the distaff, the proper arrangement of which helps to insure an even thread.

There probably were not too many spinning wheels during the early years. In 200 Essex County inventories from 1636 to 1681 spinning wheels were only listed by name in only a third. In the middle of the next century William Nelson advertised spinning wheels for sale in the Boston Gazette of October 22, 1754. In some places they were bought for $1 or $2. Benjamin Franklin choose a spinning wheel instead of a tea table as a gift for his sister in 1736.

Life was not all without fun. A country wife who lived far from neighbors would visit them, mounting a horse with the wheel tied on behind and a child in front of her. We do the same with our cars, gathering up our children to call on a nearby friend.

Some days large numbers of ladies would gather at the minister's house. While they spun he would preach a sermon to them. At one meeting there were gathered seventy flax wheels.

Rev. Amos Chase entertained sixty women and used Genesis 31:43 for his text.

So they combined religion, industry, and patriotism. Before the Revolution the Daughters of Liberty organized themselves and revolted against the Stamp Act. They pledged to wear only homespun and to drink no tea. The Boston News Letter stated on March 1, 1770 that:

"The use of the spinning wheel is now encouraged. The pernicious practise of tea-drinking is discountenanced by all ladies of the town, excepting those whose husbands are Tories."

In Northboro the ladies would give the day's work to the minister. These groups would work as a team, carding fibers, hackling flax, spinning, and reeling the yarn. While their hands were busy, their minds were being improved. Many of us would find such a day a bore, but we can also see that they must have been special occasions — these gatherings. Surely they swapped recipes and caught up on the news much as we do now.

Often their spinning matches were endurance tests whose competition could be quite keen. In 1777 Miss Eleanor Fry of East Greenwich, Rhode Island spun enough in a day for twelve linen handkerchiefs — an extraordinary achievement.

Two skeins of linen thread was a good days work. When a spinster was paid she got eight cents a day and her keep. A common weekly wage was six shillings or 95¢. However, this varied from place to place.

In 1749, 300 young spinsters, rich and poor alike, appeared on Boston Common with their wheels. This was a popular holiday recreation. But it was also most serious. In 1757 the tax on coaches and carriages was used to support a brick spinning school costing 15,000 pounds.

The story goes that in Townsend, Massachusetts a mother and her daughters in a day and a night sheared a black and a white sheep, carded a gray wool, spun, wove, cut, and made a suit of clothes for the boy who was going off to the war. Such an achievement is staggering, and probably greatly exaggerated.

It is told that Mistress Mary Prigge actually spun a pound of wool into 84,000 yards or nearly forty eight miles. This would be 150 count yarn. 80's is about the finest made today, although for exhibition purposes fine wool has been spun to more than 200 counts (200 hanks of 560 yards each in one pound of wool.)

All of this interest in spinning probably prompted the invention in 1764 of the two spindle flax wheel. By 1800 it was in common use in Scotland, although there were only a few here in America. But, according to a knowledgeable antique dealer, today we find a hundred of the others to one double flax wheel. George Washington saw fourteen girls spinning with both hands using two spindles in Boston in 1789. The flax was fastened to their waists. This was quite a feat, and undoubtedly the quality of the thread was inferior. There are many spinners today, and few, if any, can manipulate well this particular type of wheel. Carded wool or roving make it easily possible.

Joel Baldwin, of Bristol, Connecticut advertised in the Hartford Courant:

"Two handed wheels are highly recommended to young women, as they can spin faster on them."

He did not mention that in increasing the quantity the quality would suffer.

The new country was full of spinners, and by 1794 families would be spending their evenings spinning flax together. This was their "togetherness", but it was very necessary as it took five to ten spinners to keep one weaver going. In 1829, the textile manufacturers complained to Congress about the amount of spinning done at home. Gradually the machine took over, although as late as 1851 Ohio and the Western states still had a large number of spinners. But the transition from home to factory in textile manufacture took place generally speaking between 1800 and 1840.

The art of spinning almost died out, but in a few isolated corners it was still done. A friend of mine remembers her mother, Margaret Anne Tedford, spinning on her wool wheel in Nova Scotia about seventy years ago. She writes me:

"I can recall to my memory the scene when my dear mother would get out the old spinning wheel, the rolls of wool, trot back and forth and make it into yarn. However, she didn't weave, but she did make lovely hooked rugs. She made socks too for my brothers and dad. The work in those days was hard, but mother lived for others and gave all she had for ninety-two years."

Today, the art of spinning is being revived. More and more people are enjoying this ancient craft, which combines enjoyment and useful articles in one hobby.

CHAPTER III

The Spinning Wheel

BEFORE beginning to spin one must become acquainted with one's wheel, of which there are many varieties. Some old ones are still found in antique shops, and new ones are also being made.

In Europe spinning wheels were a part of the dowry and wealthy families took pride in having them made of rare woods.

The great wheel has a simple spindle and wool only is spun on it. It makes a soft yarn with easily separated fibers preferred by many. Smaller spinning wheels with the flyer and bobbin on the spindle are of two types, Saxony and Castle. The former has a slanting table and is most frequently seen. An arrangement of two levels is sometimes substituted for the slant. The Castle type is more compact with a smaller wheel. The parts are essentially the same.

Made today are spindles with flyers whose power is a small motor activated by a foot treadle. A clever man could make one to go with his wife's sewing machine.

Here are the important parts, numbering coinciding with the drawing of a Saxony type flax wheel.

1. Wheel.
2. Driving band — goes from wheel to spindle, and should be in proportion in size.

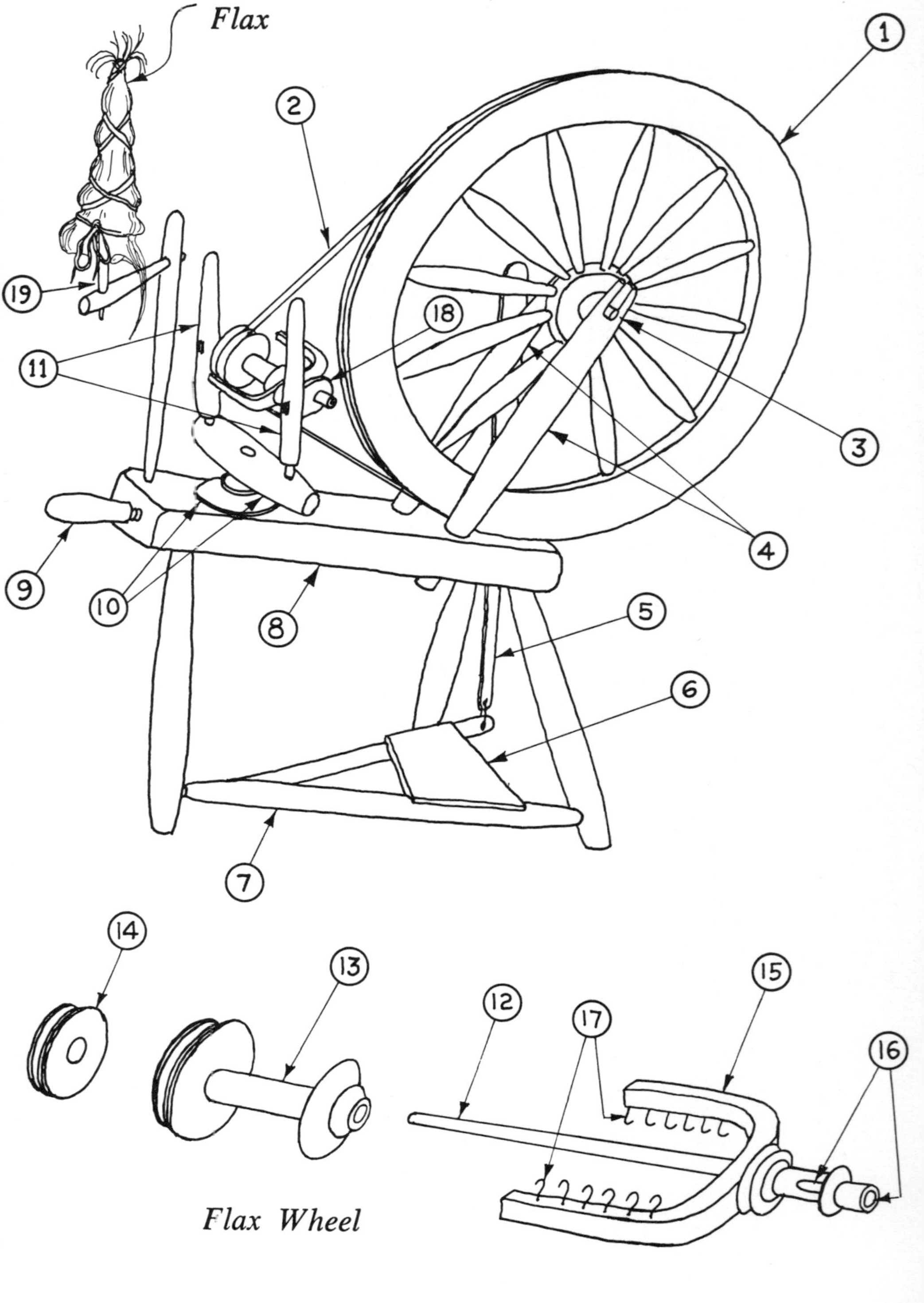

Flax Wheel

3. Axle — supports wheel in uprights, and is attached to the treadle arm. One end has a crank.
4. Uprights — support wheel.
5. Treadle arm — also called footman, and is usually wood. This hooks onto the axle and is tied to the treadle.
6. Treadle.
7. Treadle bar — attached to treadle between legs.
8. Table — supported by legs, and holds principal parts.
9. Tension screw — adjusts driving band tension.
10. Horizontal bar — also called mother-of-all. Its position is controlled by the tension screw, and thereby the driving band is tightened or loosened.
11. Spindle supports — also called maidens. The front one adjusts the spindle.
12. Spindle shaft — holds bobbin, whorl, and flyer, and has orifice at end.
13. Bobbin — has its own whorl and holds the yarn.
14. Spindle whorl — with one or two grooves. With two grooves one might find varying depths. If so, the driving band may be used in either to change the twist. If the depths are the same, the driving band on the bobbin can be placed on the empty one in order to free the spool for unwinding.
15. Flyer — also called wishbone, and aids in guiding yarn to spool.
16. Orifice or eye — at the end of the spindle. The yarn feeds through the eye to the flyer.
17. Guide hooks — on flyer, and regulate where yarn is wound on the bobbin.
18. Leather bearings — hold the spindle at each end, and are attached to the maidens.
19. Distaff — holds flax ready for spinning.

Don't forget to keep the axle and leather bearings properly lubricated. Graphite is recommended for the axle where it sets in the uprights and also where it is attached to the treadle arm. Oil or vaseline is used for the leather bearings. Don't forget the places where the treadle bar fits into the legs.

Wool Wheel Spindle Heads

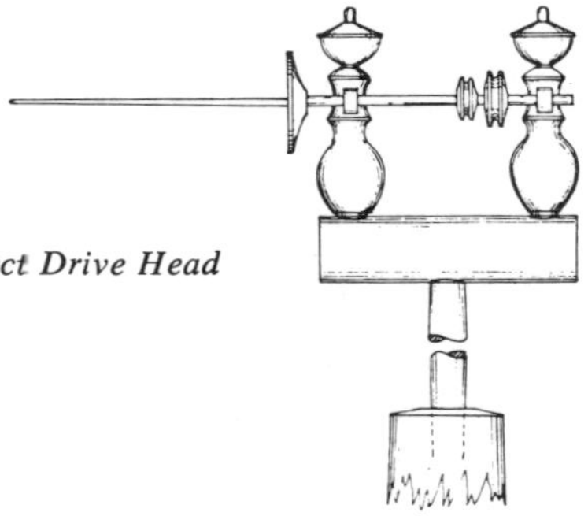

Direct Drive Head

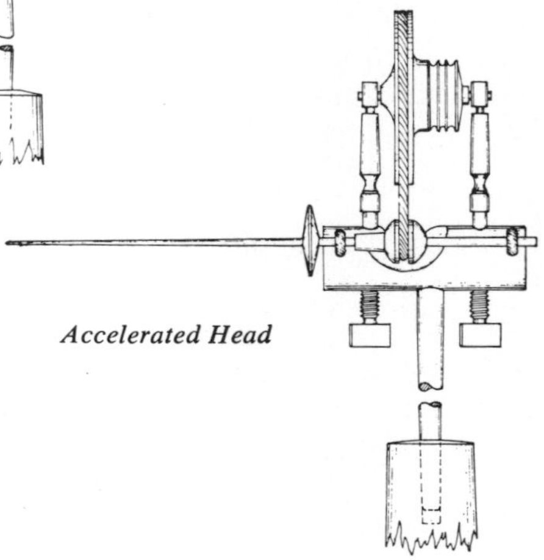

Accelerated Head

Flax Wheel Spindle and Maidens

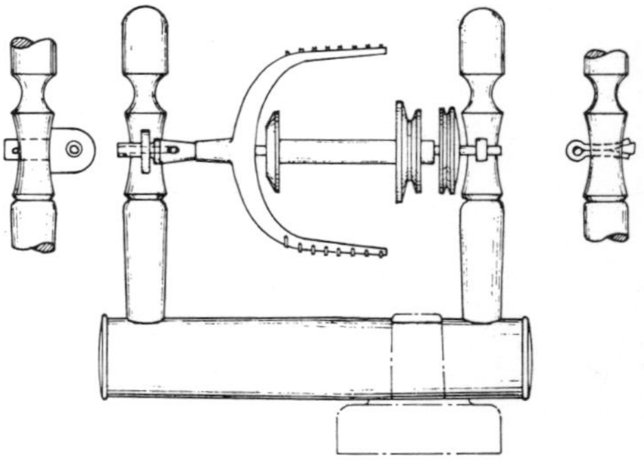

CHAPTER IV

Wool, The Miracle Fiber

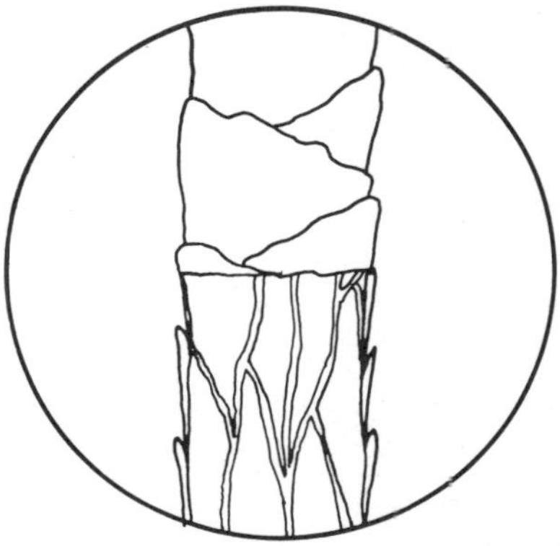

Wool Fiber

SO it was that this remarkable gift from the sheep was called by a talented spinster when she headed a group demonstration of the art of spinning at a well attended seminar at the University of Massachusetts. And indeed it is. Mother Nature has fashioned a fiber whose structure rivals any of man's inventions. Our spinning will mean more to us if we understand a bit about sheep and their wool.

The outer surface of the skin of the sheep, the epidermis, protects the inner layer which contains the important glands. The sweat glands open onto the skin surface, while the sebaceous glands open into the hair follicles. It is at this point that the wool fiber grows by adding cells which slowly extend outward. Thereby we can understand how external conditions can influence the quality and strength of the fiber. Poor diet will greatly inhibit its growth.

The sweat glands produce perspiration called suint. This combines with the more important oily material secreted by the sebaceous glands, and together they are called yolk. Where it is coagulated it resembles egg yolk which may be where the name came from. Fine wool sheep have more of this natural grease. Proper amounts of yolk help to keep the live fleece in good condition and unmatted.

There are misunderstandings about the so-called "water-proof" sheep and their natural grease. If sheep will lie down in the rain and keep still, their thick fleece will keep them dry. Yolk is not a true fat and will emulsify or break up into tiny globules in water. 4-H boys and girls are cautioned not to wash their sheep prior to showing. It is all right to do so two or three months before as it takes all this time for the fleece to be reconditioned.

Depending upon the sheep there may be from 5,000 to 50,000 wool fibers growing in a square inch of skin surface. The diameters also vary from 0.0007 to 0.0016 according to the breed. The length also has a variance of about one inch to fifteen in a year's growth. The longest fibers are used for carpet wool. Generally speaking sheep with the shorter growths will have denser and finer wool. Those with long staples will have a coarser and correspondingly less number of fibers per square inch of skin surface.

Like the skin the wool fiber has two layers of cells. The outer layer is scale-like and resembles a pine cone. These serrations as they are called are joined at the lower end, overlap, and point toward the tip. Mother Nature has very cleverly designed it thus to allow foreign matter to work out more easily. Fine wool has more serrations per square inch than coarse wool, varying from 1000 to 3000 per inch.

The second layer is called the cortex. The cortical cells are shaped like a spindle. They give the fiber strength, resilience, and elasticity. The irregular arrangement is believed by some to cause the crimp of which there are 10 to 36 per inch. It is almost impossible to destroy. The fine wools often have more. This crimp may account for one third of the total length. The fiber length is stretched as opposed to the unstretched staple length.

There may also be a medulla in the center which goes part or all the way in the fiber. This is not desirable in good wool, and is to be avoided.

The Merrimack Valley Textile Museum has a model of a wool fiber enlarged to 10,000 times. It plainly shows the scales and a cut away section shows the cortex. An enlarged view is shown here. In cross section the wool is seldom round. A square inch has a tensile strength of seventeen tons.

The characteristics of wool include its ability to absorb moisture. Under ordinary conditions it will increase 15% of its weight. In damp air it can absorb 30% to 50%. For these reasons the manufacturer must be very careful in controlling the humidity and temperature in order to insure a standardized product.

It is said that a sheep who lives a rough outdoor life will have coarse hair or kemp. Breeding plays an important part in keeping it out. Kemp is not desirable as it does not take dyes and is not strong. It is chalky white though it can be dark in a dark sheep.

It is necessary to be careful in dyeing wool which can be done at different stages. The hand spinner may be interested in "dyeing in the wool" immediately after washing. Thereby beautiful combinations of colors are produced by arranging different shades on the cards. (Mineral oil on the fingers aids the spinner using dyed wool.) Some spinners like to dye the completed skein. The manufacturers also dye right after carding and combing and in the piece of material itself. Cheapest and easiest is dyeing the finished cloth. However, there are many methods for many different effects.

Wool is a very versatile material and we must treat it with respect and understanding. In the controlled atmosphere of the factory, even after weaving, there is much more that can be done to produce a piece suited to different requirements.

Heat, moisture, and friction will interlock the fibers. This is called felting. Another step in woolen manufacture is called fulling. The cloth is shrunk and the surface is napped and sheared. The weave pattern becomes indistinct, the amount depending upon the use of the material.

One can test a wool yarn and that of other animal fibers with a match. It will smell like feathers burning, and a tiny bead comes at the end of the fiber.

As for the sheep himself, there are many, many breeds whose wool and mutton are of varying worth. Of course good breeding and feeding will help to produce both, although some are noted for certain characteristics.

The fine wool breeds include the American Merino which can give as much as 28 pounds of wool at a shearing. Hampshire and Southdown are the largest classes at the Eastern fairs. They are medium wool mutton breeds, and all purpose sheep. The Southdown has a shorter fiber length than the Hampshire. Other breeds in New England are Shropshire, Dorset, and Columbia. A long wool breed is the Lincoln sheep. The fleece may weigh as much as twenty pounds after a year's growth. The length varies from eight to twelve inches and is glossy, lustrous, and wavy.

There are seven grades of wool: fine, half blood, three-eighths blood, quarter blood, low quarter blood, common, and braid. Most braid wool is lustrous, and comes from the long wool breeds such as the Lincoln. American Merino is a fine grade. Hampshire is three eighths and quarter blood.

Wool is called also according to the spinning count. This count is based on the number of hanks, 560 yards in length, which can be spun from a pound of wool. For example, the fine wool of the American Merino is 64's and 80's. The Hampshire is 50's and 56's, while the Lincoln with its long and coarser fiber is 36's and 40's.

Shearing is done in the spring, though some parts of the country do it twice a year. Sometimes it is done shortly before lambing at which time great care must be taken. A shearer who cuts his hands will heal quickly due to the healing qualities in the wool grease. He can also shear 100 to 150 sheep in a day.

Those who shear find it much harder on a cold day as the grease builds up on the blades. Many herd their animals close together to induce perspiration. The suint will then soften the yolk and shearing will be facilitated.

A ewe from two to three years old produces the best wool, and there is a marked decline after seven years. An average weight of a fleece is under ten pounds.

The Angora goat produces mohair also used in materials. Mohair should be mixed with wool in hand spinning.

CHAPTER V

Fleece to Yarn -- How to Spin

IT takes a great deal of experience to adequately know how to judge fleeces. But there are a few guide lines by which the novice can go. A good fleece comes from a well cared for sheep that has had a proper diet all year around. Take a lock, snap it back and forth. If it breaks half of the way down, the diet was poor half of the way in the growing season. 4-H clubbers take pride in raising fine animals. The ones that are shown at fairs will have shorter fleeces due to clipping and grooming. Sheep should be shorn by an expert who will take the fleece in one piece with no "second cuts" which destroy the good fiber length. Avoid wool which has mildewed.

Next comes sorting out the fleece. Lay some papers down on the kitchen or basement floor. Spread out the whole fleece. Discard obviously dirty hind end and badly matted areas, such as come from underneath. Pull out burrs, etcetera in the direction of the tip of the lock if possible. Sort according to quality. The best comes from the shoulders and sides. Good wool and good mutton come from the same part of the sheep. Good authorities say that it is best kept unwashed.

Some spinners prefer to spin "in the grease," but I think a minimum of washing is helpful. This is a matter of opinion, and is up to the individual to decide. Knowing the construction of the fiber and the fact that it will felt under the situation of heat, moisture, and pressure, we consider carefully how we do it. A little experimenting should be done on a small quantity, since each one of us would probably have different equipment. I took four old diapers (old muslin curtains would be better), and made bags which can hold ¼ of a pound of wool. They can be closed at the top with an elastic, or tied with a string.

The following directions are for a top loading automatic washing machine which at some point in the cycle can provide cold water. The principals can be adapted for hand use. However, the final spin is most helpful. A thorough understanding of the machine is necessary, as it is not allowed to follow its usual cycle.

In a top loading automatic washing machine, cover the bags with cold water. Do not agitate, but slosh gently by hand. Spin out the water. Remove bags and make a cold sudsy solution. A detergent for cold water is available. Replace the bags and slosh gently by hand in the suds. Let them soak ten or fifteen minutes. Spin out the water. Cover again with cold water. Slosh gently by hand. Spin out the water. Remove the wool from the bags and spread it out to dry.

Some prefer warm water and mild soap. A constant temperature must be maintained. If you wash by hand in a tub or basin, squeeze the water out gently.

Rubbing and agitation with hot water will felt the wool. Matted wool means more difficult carding, which can be a chore anyway. The lanolin should not be all washed out. If it is, or you are using machine prepared wool, a little mineral oil on the fingers will facilitate spinning. Others sprinkle olive oil on and tease it through the wool.

When the wool is dry, it should be teased or gently pulled apart to fluff the fibers and allow all possible foreign pieces to drop out. Those with plenty of time and strong shoulders will want to card their wool, although some feel that it weakens the fibers. It weakens the shoulders anyway! There is, however, a small home carding machine, cranked by hand which does about three pounds an hour. By using cards, effects other than those of plain wool yarn may be obtained. I have seen the most beautiful blue-green heather yarn created by carding dyed wool. A touch of black was used to soften it. Of course there are many combinations of colors that can be used if you "dye in the wool". Different fibers, including mohair, angora, and other animal hair, can also be mixed.

Carding

Cards are like paddles with bent wires set into them. It is recommended that a new pair be marked Left and Right.

Evenly spread a thin layer of wool on the teeth of the left one, whose handle points away from you. With the handle of the right card pointed toward you (see illustration above), lightly press the two cards together, teeth meeting teeth, and draw the card in the right hand toward you. Brush the wool in this manner several times, then return the wool to the card in the left hand. This can be done very easily by holding the handles of both cards in the same direction and drawing them away from each other. Repeat this entire operation several times until the wool is a soft, fluffy roll and falls easily from the cards. This roll of wool is called a rolag. You may wish to vary this procedure.

Those of you who eliminate this process need to tease the wool until all matted areas are out. With care a most respectable yarn can spun. Some feel a few irregularities give it character.

Before even attempting to spin, it is wise to practice pedalling. This looks so easy, but achieving a steady gait does take a little practice. The action is so different from our accelerator pedal, which only goes down to make speed. To get the general idea of the action, put two balls of yarn in a couple of bags or jars and ply them. Plying instructions come later. Start pedalling with the axle crank at the top. Make sure it goes in a clockwise direction. Slowing up will send the wheel backwards, and the yarn is in a mess.

Let's go back to early man and his first attempts at spinning. Take the raw wool and draw out a few fibers two or three inches. Twist it with your fingers. There is your yarn, but of course it will unwind easily. But you will get the idea of what the thickness of the unspun fibers should be to make the yarn you want. The novice will do well to practice on medium length wool.

If you can obtain a spindle, it is advantageous to learn on this, as its operation does not require synchronizing both feet and hands. Approximate dimensions are as follows: A ⅜" dowel, 18 inches long has a 3 inch diameter whorl, ¾ inch thick, 2½ inches from the bottom. A notch is at the top of the dowel to hold the yarn in a half hitch. Please note the illustration.

Tie some ready spun wool 18 inches long just above the top of the whorl. Pass it under the whorl, around the end of the dowel and up to the top where it is half hitched. Pull out some raw wool, and lap it over the end of the wool about four inches. Hold this join with the right hand and spin the spindle clockwise with the left. Notice how the twist goes up the yarn. With the left hand hold the end of the twisted wool and pull out or draft more with the right. Release the left hand to allow the twist to go up. Be sure the spindle has not stopped. Continue spinning and drafting, the hands moving along rhythmically. When the yarn is long, and the spindle is almost to the floor, hold the spindle securely, undo the half hitch and wind all the yarn in a figure of eight above the whorl. Leave enough to go under again and up for the half hitch with a few inches to spare.

Those who wish to start spinning on the wheel will profit with a helper who can turn the wheel very slowly. Take about 18 inches of yarn and tie it securely to the bobbin. Wind a few rounds to stop it from slipping. Pass it over a guide hook, through the eye and out the end. A bent paper clip helps to pull it through the orifice.

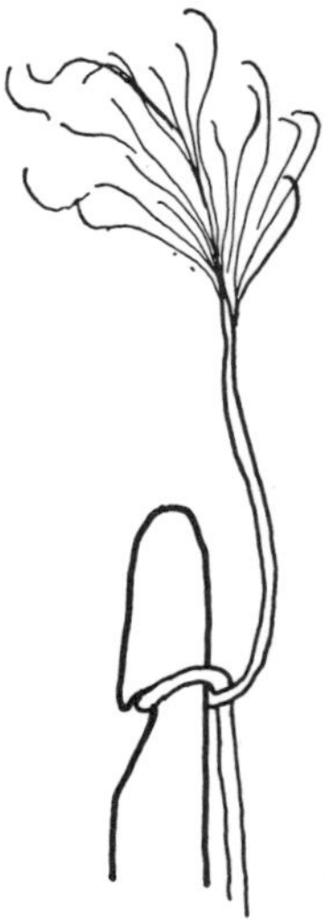

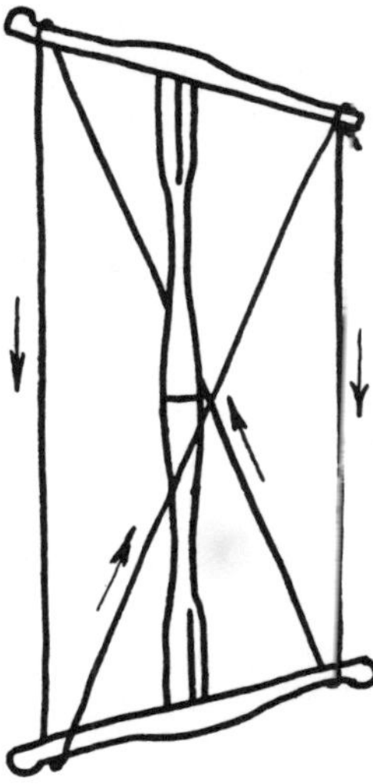

Niddy Noddy

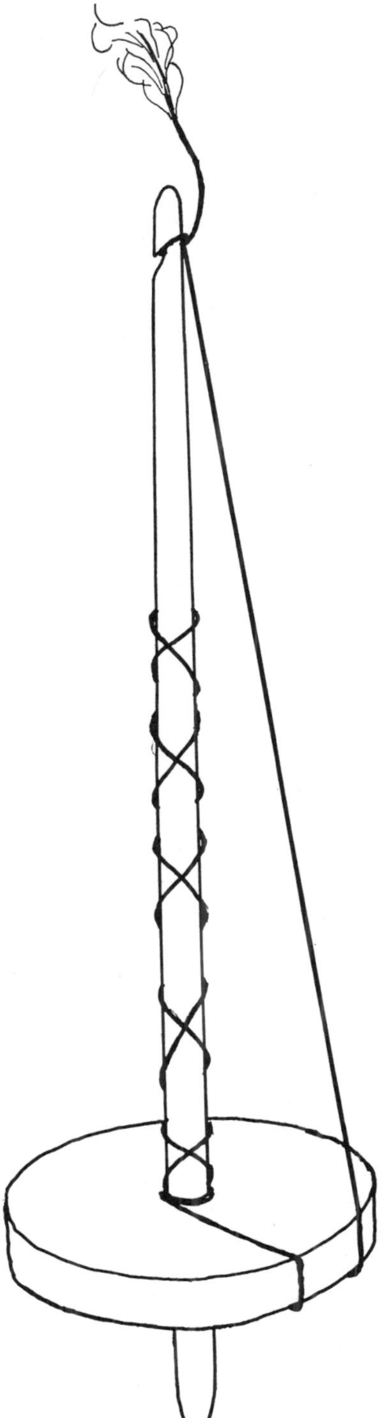

Hand Spindle

The process continues much as spindle spinning. The end of yarn is held straight out from the orifice. Draft a few inches of raw wool and lap it onto the yarn. Start pedalling easily with the axle crank at the top and the wheel going in a clockwise direction. Be sure to hold the mass of wool so that the twist will not reach it. The right hand drafts the wool and the left holds firmly on the yarn. When the wool is drafted, the left hand releases the yarn to allow the twist to continue and produce yarn. When it is necessary to stop, wind the yarn and mass of wool around one of the maidens to prevent unnecessary untwisting. Before starting to pedal again have a few inches drafted ready for twisting.

The action of the driving band on the bobbin whorl will pull the yarn onto the spool. The tension will need to be adjusted and the spinner can tell this herself. If it is too loose, the yarn will not wind on, but will twist too hard and create knots. As one part of the spool fills, move the yarn to the next guide hook. Make sure the yarn does not get caught on the hooks.

Most people hold the yarn and wool straight out from the orifice. Others feel that the method used on the older wool wheels is better for the wool which is drawn out and twisted at right angles to the orifice. Then after a few inches are done, it is brought around to the front and fed in. Apparently there is less strain when the winding on the spool and twisting are not simultaneous. Feeding it directly is known as the worsted method, while the other is used for woolen materials. See the Glossary of Terms for a description of each.

DON'T GIVE UP!

When the bobbin is full, release it and rewind the yarn to a niddy-noddy or similar skeining device. If it has been spun tightly, it will be knotty (naughty is right!). Upon removing from the winder, tie the two ends together. Keep the yarn at an even tension on the whole skein. With yarn of another color loosely tie around the skein in three places to keep it in order.

Yarn left on a niddy-noddy will tend to unkink in time. But to hasten the process, remove it from the winder, dampen the skein thoroughly in cold water, or wash it carefully if necessary. Squeeze gently. Hang it up to dry on a rod with a weight on it. Never change the temperature of water when washing wool.

Now we have achieved a single yarn. This can be used by weavers for weft, and if spun hard and care is used it will do for warp yarn. Knitters disagree strongly on using single or two ply yarn. Knit some of each and make your own choice. It is well to wash it before knitting to minimize shrinking.

To ply, take two balls of yarn and place them in jars. Paper bags will do. Tie the two ends to the starting yarn which goes from spool to flyer and through the orifice. Guide the knot past the guide hooks. To start pedalling, the axle crank should be slightly to the left of top center. This will make the wheel go in a counter-clockwise direction when pedalled. (Usually yarn is spun with the wheel going in a clockwise direction). Upon the twist will depend the need for another stretching.

You may find it easier to reverse the position of your hands as suggested above. Of course this is true of many hand motions. Do what is comfortable for you. A rough fiber like wool is easier to spin than the smooth fibers such as linen, cotton and silk. Short wool needs more thorough teasing and carding, and is harder to spin.

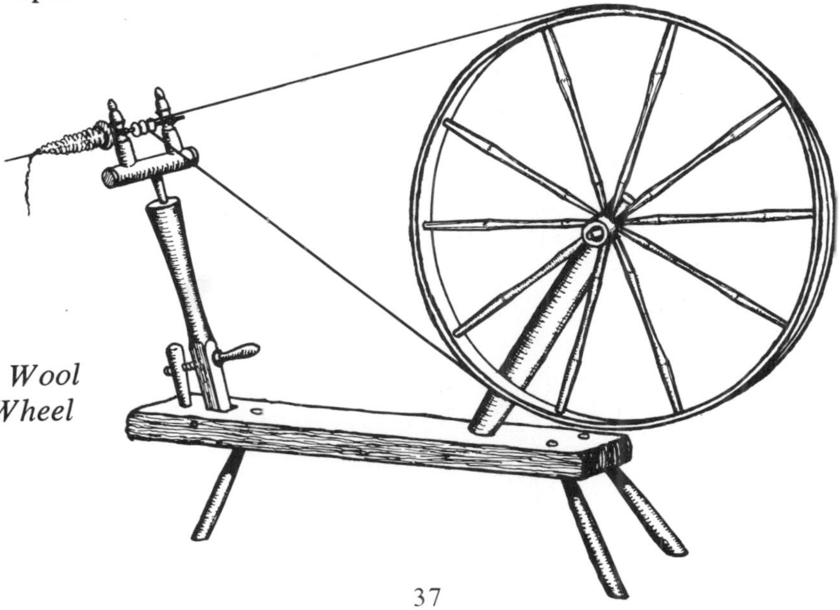

Wool Wheel

CHAPTER VI

Places to Visit

Only a few short years ago when this little book was first printed, the art of spinning was seldom shown. Now there are many historical places where the old textile arts are practised and demonstrated. Members of the A.A.A. will find their tour guides listing places where spinning and weaving are featured. The potential traveler would do well to join. The Chambers of Commerce in many cities provide helpful information. There are also many active organizations and local newspapers will tell of craft exhibits and demonstrations. Before planning any trips it is wise to check ahead to make sure the museums will be open on the day you wish to visit. Following are a few of the many places that are interesting and informative.

CONNECTICUT
- Mystic, Mystic Seaport

GEORGIA
- Atlanta, Tullie Smith House Restoration
- Lumpkin, Westville

INDIANA
- Noblesville, Conner Prairie Pioneer Settlement

KENTUCKY
- Berea, Berea College Appalachian Museum
- Pleasant Hill, Shakertown

MAINE
- Poland Spring, The United Society of Shakers, The Shaker Museum, Sabbathday Lake

MARYLAND
- Westminster, Carroll County Farm Museum

MASSACHUSETTS
- North Andover, Merrimack Valley Textile Museum
- Plymouth, Harlow Old-Fort House
- Sturbridge, Old Sturbridge Village

MICHIGAN
- Dearborn, Greenfield Village

MISSOURI
- Branson, Silver Dollar City
- St. Louis, The Old Court House

NEW HAMPSHIRE
- Portsmouth, Strawbery Banke

NEW YORK
- Cooperstown, The Farmers' Museum
- Monroe, Old Museum Village of Smith's Clove

NORTH CAROLINA
- Blue Ridge Parkway, Mile 238.5, Brinegar Cabin
  Mile 294, Parkway Craft Center
- Winston-Salem, Old Salem

OHIO
- Bath, Hale Farm and Western Reserve Village
- Columbus, Ohio Historical Center
- Piqua, Picqua Historical Area
- West Liberty, The C. S. Smucker Family

OREGON
- Aurora, The Ox Barn

PENNSYLVANIA
- Ambridge, Old Economy Village
- Lancaster, Pennsylvania Farm Museum of Landis Valley
- Soudersburg, Mill Bridge Craft Village
- Stroudsburg, Quiet Valley Farm Museum

RHODE ISLAND
- Pawtucket, Old Slater Mill

VIRGINIA
- Williamsburg, Colonial Williamsburg

WASHINGTON, D.C.
- Museum of History and Technology of the Smithsonian

WEST VIRGINIA
- Harman, The Old Mill

CANADA, Ontario
- Lang, Century Village
- Morrisburg, Upper Canada Village
- Toronto, Black Creek Pioneer Village

CHAPTER VII

Where to Get Equipment, Materials, Etc.

The following places are a few of the many who now carry supplies for the spinner as well as the weaver. Your local craft organization can also be helpful. It is always appreciated when the person you write to knows where you read about his services.

BARTLETTYARNS, INC.
Harmony, Maine 04942
This company carries hand cards, drop spindles, a drum carder, different types of rovings, etc. in addition to supplies for weavers. Send 25c to cover postage and please mention what your particular needs are.

CASA DE LAS TEJEDORAS
1619 East Edinger
Santa Ana, California 92705
Available are individually handcrafted spindles, niddy noddies, and tapestry combs in beautiful woods, as well as prepared fibers for spinning, looms and yarns for weaving.

EDGERTON'S HANDCRAFTS
210 West Town Street
Norwich, Connecticut 06360
Mrs. Edgerton has an agency for Leclerc looms and carries Putnam dyes and books on textile crafts. Classes are held in weaving, spinning and natural dyeing. Please send self-addressed stamped envelope for further information.

Frederick J. Fawcett, Inc.
129 South Street
Boston, Massachusetts 02111
In addition to the large assortment of linen for weavers, they carry flax fiber for spinners.

E. B. Frye & Son, Inc.
Wilton, New Hampshire 03086
Makers of hand cards, they will send information on the different types made with their prices upon receipt of a self-addressed stamped envelope.

Haltec Corporation
32123 Winona Road, Dept. M.
Winona, Ohio 44493
This company makes a Saxony type reproduction of an early American spinning wheel in kit form. All parts are solid maple and are turned, drilled, and ready for assembly. A branch type flax distaff and niddy noddy are also available. Write for free colored brochure.

Handcraft Wools — Ted Carson
Box 738
Streetsville, Ontario, Canada L5M 2B9
Mr. Carson has available an excellent selection of supplies for the spinner, weaver, and dyer.

Harrisville Designs
Harrisville, New Hampshire 03450
For the spinner who needs to save time in dyeing and carding a fleece, this firm has a wide range of colors including natural shades in carded wool. They also have looms. Please send 50c for complete sample.

The Meyer Company
P.O. Box 6664
Seattle, Washington 98116
Send a self-addressed stamped envelope for information about their drum carder.

Robin and Russ Handweavers
533 North Adams Street
McMinnville, Oregon 97128
Their supplies for spinners are very complete, including

wheels, hand spindles, wool cards, drum carders, usually Romney and Corriedale fleeces and other fibers. For weavers they have yarns and looms.

Mr. and Mrs. David A. Pennington
1993 West Liberty
Ann Arbor, Michigan 48103

This couple have a very thorough knowledge of the many types of old wheels. If you have an unusual one, send a picture and/or rubbing of the design, numbers, or lettering. A self-addressed stamped envelope is always appreciated. They also teach and demonstrate many old crafts and sell supplies for spinning and dyeing.

Sheepman Supply Company
Route 1, Box 141
Barboursville, Virginia 22923

Starting with sheep at age thirteen, Mr. Hess, the owner, has been awarded the Ford Motor Company's Sheep Efficiency Award of 1970. His catalog lists items useful for the everyday sheep raiser. For hand spinners he offers raw fleeces, a Saxony type wheel, and cards.

Shuttle, Spindle & Dyepot
998 Farmington Avenue
West Hartford, Connecticut 06107

This quarterly magazine is highly recommended and is devoted to all the textile crafts. It is a publication of the Handweavers Guild of America, Inc.

Paula Simmons
Box 12
Suquamish, Washington 98392

One of the outstanding spinners in the United States, Mrs. Simmons has her own black sheep from which she spins yarn and weaves fabrics. She has for sale reprints of her magazine articles, spinning oil, and sample cards of her handspun yarn. She has no shop, but sells by mail. If you would like a free price list, please send a stamped self-addressed envelope.

Spincraft
Box 332
Richardson, Texas 75080

Their leaflet is furnished without charge and describes hand crafted items made to order. Listed are spinning wheels, hand spindles, cards, books on spinning and flax.

TRADITIONAL HANDCRAFTS
John and Gloria Teeter
571 Randolph Street
Northville, Michigan 48167
The Teeters are handling a comprehensive line of supplies for spinning, weaving, dyeing and macrame. They also give lessons and demonstrations. Send a legal size self-addressed stamped envelope for their catalog.

THE UNICORN, CRAFT AND HOBBY BOOK SERVICE
P.O. Box 645
Rockville, Maryland 20851
Their catalog has around a thousand titles, many of which have very helpful reviews. Please send 25c, refundable on the first purchase.

THE UNITED SOCIETY OF SHAKERS
The Shaker Museum
Sabbathday Lake
Poland Spring, Maine 04274
This museum is publishing *American Spinning Wheels* by David A. Pennington and Michael Taylor. The book is without question the most complete ever written in the field of American spinning wheels. Send a self-addressed stamped envelope for more information and the price.

CHAPTER VIII

Glossary of Terms

CARDING — The fluffing of wool and fiber separation is done on two cards or carders which have many small teeth as in a brush. They are bent as can be seen in the illustration on page 31. Small hand carding machines are available to those who wish to prepare a great deal of wool.

CLOCK REEL — After the wool was spun it was reeled, sometimes onto spokes on the wheel itself, a niddy-noddy, or in later days a clock reel which clicked when 40 revolutions had been made. The distance around was two yards. 80 yards was called a knot, and seven knots made a skein or hank.

COMBING — After carding the wool is drawn through a comb which straightens out the fibers and removes the short fibers preparatory to commercial worsted spinning. This can be done by the hand spinner also.

DISTAFF — The word itself is from the Anglo-Saxon, "dis" = flax and "staef" = stick. This device holds the flax ready for spinning. See the illustration of the spinning wheel (part number 19). The proper arrangement of the fibers will help to determine the quality of the yarn. There is no practical advantage in putting wool on a distaff.

DRAFT — Before the wool is twisted, the fibers are drawn out or attenuated to the proper amount for required thickness of the desired yarn. The drawing out is called drafting, and the amount drawn is the draft. This is not a common term.

HACKLE — These wicked looking devices are found in antique shops. There are different spellings and pronunciations of this word: hackle, heckle, hatchel, hetchel, etc. In the preparation of flax the hackle is used in hackling or splitting the fibers. A hackle is a board with long steel teeth set closely together through which the flax is drawn. (See illustration.) To obtain a finer material a series of hackles are used. The set of the teeth is nearer together on each succeeding hackle. This straightens, cleans, and separates the line fiber from short flax fiber or tow.

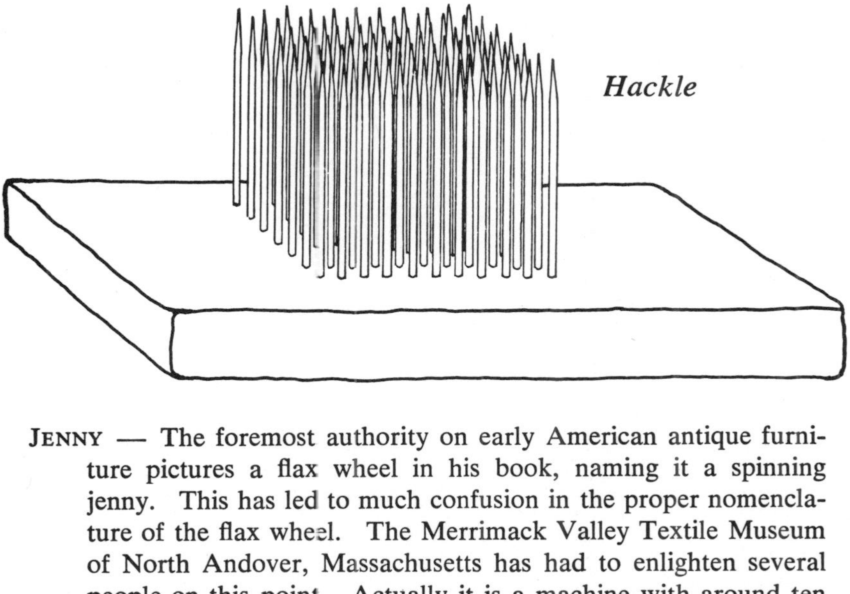

Hackle

JENNY — The foremost authority on early American antique furniture pictures a flax wheel in his book, naming it a spinning jenny. This has led to much confusion in the proper nomenclature of the flax wheel. The Merrimack Valley Textile Museum of North Andover, Massachusetts has had to enlighten several people on this point. Actually it is a machine with around ten upright spindles turned by means of drum-driven-bands. One hand controlled a travelling carriage which fed the yarn onto the bobbin after the roving had been spun. The other turned a wheel whose motion resulted in turning the spindles. Wool rovings were previously prepared for use. James Hargreaves patented it in 1770.

Kemp — Poorly bred sheep will sometimes have in their fleece this coarse hair called kemp. It is chalky white and will not take dyes. Since it is also brittle and weak it is very unacceptable in a fleece.

Lanolin — This is the refined yolk or wool grease. It is extracted from the fleece by centrifugal force or by chemical means. Lanolin is widely used pharmaceutically.

Linsey-woolsey — This is cloth made of wool and linen as the name implies. Using the linen as the warp where strength was needed it had been woven since the Middle Ages. Cotton took its place in the early 1800's when that material was being produced by factories in desirable strength for warp. Some of the early quilted coverlets are erroneously called linsey-woolsey. Close analysis shows that they are entirely of wool. The Winterthur Museum collection has six of these. Other coverlets in their collection which probably date in the 19th century are woven with cotton weft and a woolen warp. Competent authorities have not found as yet an early fabric with a wool warp and a linen weft.

Mule — In 1779 Samuel Crompton, using ideas of Hargreaves' jenny and Arkwright's water frame, invented a spinning machine which he called a mule because it was a cross between these two. It still had the intermittent motion of the great wheel, however.

Niddy-noddy — A look at the illustration will demonstrate the little poem. "Niddy-noddy. Two heads and one body." This is a very simple device for winding yarn. Unlike the clock reel one would have to count the times around to determine the length. One end of one arm allows the skein to be taken off easily.

Noils — In the process of commercial or hand combing, short fibers are removed. These noils are due to "second cut" shearing, poor diet of the sheep causing breakage, and carding. They are used in commercial woolen spinning.

Rolag — The neat roll of wool which comes from the hand card is called a rolag.

Roving — Immediately prior to spinning the wool has been drawn out to a reduced size, continuous length called a roving.

Sliver — This is a continuous ropelike material in one of the stages preliminary to commercial spinning.

Staple — The staple is a lock or group of wool fibers. When it is stretched the fiber length can be determined. The staple length is measured when the wool is unstretched.

Suint — This is the perspiration secreted by the sweat glands which combines with the yolk.

Top — In the preparation of yarn for commercial worsted spinning, the wool is combed and made into a thick, long, fibered strand, ropelike in form. This is wound into a large ball called top.

Woolen — In woolen spinning the fibers have not been combed and are not as straight as in worsted spinning. See the illustration. There is a higher proportion of air to wool, and the yarn is softer and bulky. The cloth manufactured is warm, and can have a fuzzy surface in which the weave does not show.

Worsted — Worstead, England gives us the name for this well known yarn and cloth. Combing produces a parallel fibered

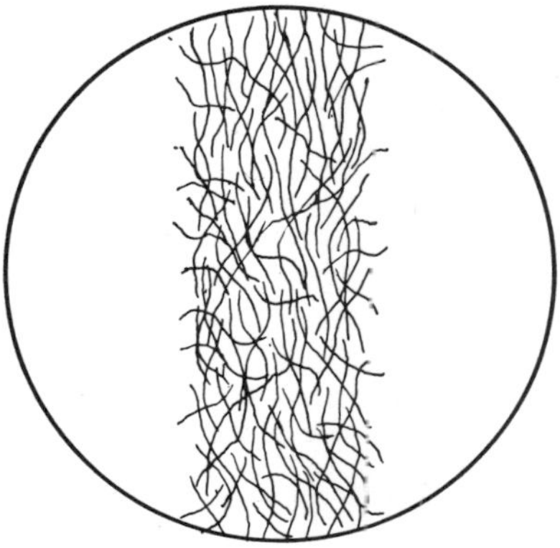

Woolen Sliver

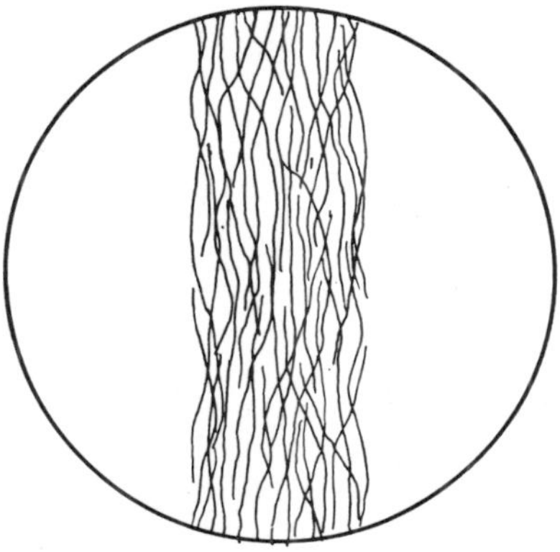

Worsted Sliver

yarn. See the illustration. Wool for combing should be at least two inches long. Four or five is even better. The longer fibers produce lustrous and glossy wool. When the yarn is spun it is twisted harder than woolen yarn. The material itself is generally firm and smooth. The weave shows, and it does not drape as easily as woolen material.

YARN COUNT — The English or Bradford system of terming yarn is based on the number of hanks 560 yards in length that can be spun from a pound of wool. This is not an absolute measurement. It goes from about 36's to 80's.

YOLK — The sebaceous glands open into the hair follicles and secrete the wool grease which combines with the suint from the sweat glands. This combination is called yolk. The refined product lanolin has many important uses. On the sheep it helps to keep his fleece in good condition.